The Naked I: Wide Open

Created by
20% Theatre Company Twin Cities
based on the stories of over 20 transgender and
gender non-conforming
artists and allies

Inspired by
The Naked I: Monologues from Beyond the Binary
by Tobias K. Davis
(*www.tobiaskdavis.com*)

The Naked I: Wide Open received its World Premiere at Intermedia
Arts in Minneapolis, MN, in February 2012. The production included
over 50 performers, directors, designers, and technical staff.

Front Cover Design by Tracy Lee (www.tracyleedesign.com).
Back Cover Photograph by Anna Min/MIN Enterprises (www.minenterprises.com).
Cover and Interior Layout by Alyx J. Hanson (www.alyxjhanson.com).
Edited by Claire Avitabile, Anthony Neuman, and Alyx J. Hanson.

For Toby –
Here's to making magic
and changing the world!

Notes on Character:

This Play can be performed by as few as five actors, to as many as 30 or more. Ideally, performers will represent gender identities as diverse as the characters in the Play do, but by no means is it necessary for a performer to identify the same as a character they are portraying.

Notes on Staging:

The Naked I: Wide Open was created with minimalism in mind – no fancy sets or costumes here, just a few chairs and props as needed. All that matters are the stories, and the individuals telling them. These pieces can – and should – be performed not only in conventional theatre venues, but unconventional ones as well – such as schools, coffee shops, business establishments, churches, etc.

Stage directions are present merely to serve as a guide, or to share how a piece was staged in the world premiere. Producers should in no way feel they have to follow any of the stage directions.

Notes on Voiceovers:

Several shorter pieces in *The Naked I: Wide Open* were performed as pre-recorded voiceovers that were played during set changes between longer pieces. Producers may feel free to have these shorter pieces performed live.

Acknowledgements:

20% Theatre Company Twin Cities would like thank:

Tobias K. Davis, Claire Avitabile, Blythe Davis, Nicole Wilder, Anthony Neuman, Shannon Hessburg, Sam Kunz, Miles Zane Bard, Renata Shaffer-Gottschalk, Megan Lembke, Erica Fields, Meggie Greivell, Derek Ewing, LJ Johnson, Ariel Leaf, Lindsey Cacich, Esme Rodriguez, Meghan Gunderson, MaryLynn Mennicke, Kris Gebhard, Katie Starks, JL Mohnkern, AP Looze, Meredith Larson, Neil Schneider, Mame Pelletier, Mykel Pennington, JamieAnn Meyers, Jenn Western, Katie Burgess, Zealot Hamm, Ana Hagedorn, Jen Tuder, Lucas Scheelk, Ben Resman, Kelly Waterman, Davey Ethan Wilkes, Abel Knochel, Remy Corso, Walken Schweigert, Maria "Mea" Johnson, Jay Masika, Tom Glaser, Cheré Suzette Bergeron, Melanie Williams, Jessamine Bristow, Anika Reitman, Kaitlyn Andrews, Meg Brown, Miranda Foslien, L Puck Matz, Gabe Moses, Jaime Hokanson, Ethan Turcotte, Andrea Jenkins, Ethan Lyn Draeger, Alyx J. Hanson, Jessica Englund, Lane McKiernan, Rebecca Lawrence, Troy Osswald, Kelli Gorr, TJ Kampa, Ruth Virkus, Danielle Siver, Ann Lindstrom, Shannon Forney, Anya Kremenetsky, Philanthrofund Foundation, the Transgender Commission and the Women's Student Activist Collective at the University of Minnesota, Pangea World Theatre, Red Card Production, HOMOapolis.com, Minneapolis Public Libraries, TransParentDay.org, Theatre Space Project, Bedlam Theatre, Elpis Enterprises, Gadfly Theatre Productions, Dr. Paul Reitman, Jake Davis and Intermedia Arts, and the more than 1,000 audience members who sold-out the world premiere.

ACT ONE

NAKED

created by Claire Avitabile, with contributions from Linda Sue Anderson, Adam Arnold, Erin Carlson, Alexis Clarksean, Chris Durant, Kelli Gorr, Marie Halverson, Jay Hemenway, Christine Johnson, Danielle Kiminski, Kari Elizabeth Kjeldseth, Ariel Leaf, AP Looze, Lane McKiernan, Anthony Neuman, Samantha Oestreicher, Mykel Pennington, Ben Resman, Amy Salloway, Walken Schweigert, Renata Shaffer-Gottschalk, and Davey Ethan Wilkes

ONE: Origin before 900

TWO: Middle English and Old English

THREE: Meaning:

FOUR: not covered by clothing

FIVE: scantily supplied or furnished, lacking embellishment

SIX: devoid of concealment or disguise

SEVEN: lacking confirmation or support

EIGHT: unaided by any optical device or instrument – such as, quote: "the naked eye"

NINE: Synonyms:

TEN: uncovered

ELEVEN: unarmed

TWELVE: undisguised

THIRTEEN: nude

FOURTEEN:	stripped
FIFTEEN:	peeled
THREE:	raw
TWO:	open
NINE:	direct
EIGHT:	evident
FIVE:	outspoken
SIX:	honest
SEVEN:	exposed
FOUR:	vulnerable
ONE:	Naked
ELEVEN:	I feel naked.
TWELVE:	I feel naked.
EIGHT:	So do I.
FOURTEEN:	Every day.
TWO:	All the time.
NINE:	I feel the most naked when it doesn't make sense to be naked.
THIRTEEN:	When I'm exposed to a world I'm not supposed to be living in.
FOURTEEN:	When I cry in front of someone for the first time.
SIX:	When I am actually naked,
EIGHT:	and alone.

SEVEN:	When all I want is to feel loved, but all someone else wants is to fuck me.
FIFTEEN:	When forgetting to take my pills becomes a habit.
TEN:	When someone calls me "sir" and then soon realizes or thinks they made a mistake.
FIVE:	I feel the most naked when I let her fuck me, because I never used to let anyone fuck me. Ever. I was always on top, in charge, in control and responsible for the pleasure of the other. I wasn't supposed to be wanted by another. I feel the most naked when I am naked. When I give the control away.
ONE:	I feel the most naked when I am truly naked, and have to come face to face with a body that is so unattractive by any American cultural standards. A body that, despite all my attempts at size acceptance and fat activism and radical self-love and feminist readings and theories and positive media choices...I loathe. Vehemently, and viciously.
TWO:	I feel the most naked when I am fully dressed and yet ashamed.
EIGHT:	When I don't like what I see in the mirror.
THREE:	When I have uncomfortable clothes on.
FOUR:	Or when I actually answer with the truth when someone asks
FIVE:	"How are you?"
FOURTEEN:	Instead of saying what we've all been conditioned to say:
ELEVEN:	"Fine thanks, how are you?"

SEVEN:	I feel the most naked when I let someone read my writing.
EIGHT:	When I step onto a stage.
THIRTEEN:	When I'm watching a play that I directed.
NINE:	When I share my art with someone. Or everyone.
FOURTEEN:	I feel the most naked when I get so angry that the anger takes over and I begin to lose control.
FIFTEEN:	Everything that's on the inside is suddenly on the outside...
TEN:	I'm completely vulnerable and there's nowhere to hide.
TWELVE:	I feel the most naked when I'm practicing yoga!

(other performers laugh, then realize the sincerity of what TWELVE is saying)

TWELVE:	I can't hide from myself when I am on my mat. Everything is revealed, every fear, every insecurity.
SIX:	I feel the most naked when I can't protect my own boundaries.
ELEVEN:	When I remember the abuse of my past.
FIFTEEN:	When I remember...
FOUR:	And feel ashamed of it.
SEVEN:	Or angry at myself for feeling ashamed...
FOURTEEN:	I feel the most naked when I have to tell someone that they have hurt me. When I expose my feelings in any way.

TEN:	When I try to share stories about my childhood and am met with shocked silence.
EIGHT:	I feel the most naked when I'm trying to explain my life to a total stranger.
ONE:	Or when I'm fucking a total stranger!
SIX:	Someone whose name I don't even know...
THREE:	...Or have forgotten by the time we took our clothes off.
ONE:	*(slowly seducing an audience member)* When I'm almost entirely clothed, harness pulled tight, and you – stripped to nothing but heels in front of me.
EIGHT:	After incredible sex... when I fear I might fall in love with this person.
TWELVE:	Or after really bad sex... when I just want to get out of there but I cannot find my underpants.
NINE:	I feel naked in doctor's offices, even the ones where they let me keep my clothes on.
TWO:	The vulnerable naked, the powerless naked, the "we know better than you about what your body does, is, or means so just shut up and take it" naked.
SIX:	"Get out of our space and feel shame" naked.
THREE:	"And if you don't we will render you invisible" naked.
SIX:	"Outcast" naked.
FIVE:	My "girl parts" never figured out quite how to work right, and now every time I see a doctor they have to "feel out the problem".

FIFTEEN:	I hate this, and it hurts, but I'm 25 years in to my life and the only option left is to get everything taken out.
FIVE:	No womb, no ovaries.
FIFTEEN:	Will I still be a woman?
FIVE:	Or feel like a woman?
THIRTEEN:	I feel the most naked when I don't know what to do next.
ELEVEN:	All the signs point in different directions.
THIRTEEN:	When I can't make a decision.
ELEVEN:	When everyone is waiting for me, expecting things from me.
FOURTEEN:	The pressure –
THREE:	is too much.
TWO:	I feel the most naked when I realize that I actually was wrong. Really wrong.
FOUR:	And all I want to do is make it right.
TWO:	When I've had a fight with my lover and I'm ready to stop being mad and all I want more than anything, ever, is a hug, and the comfort of their arms, and I'm feeling too proud to ask...
THIRTEEN:	...but then I do.
TWELVE:	Or when I've had a fight with *my* lover - when flirtation goes awry, becomes conflict, turns to combustion, and there I stand with a broken hearted hard-on,
THREE:	trying to find the spot they left unlocked.

6

FIVE: I feel the most naked when I am the fattest person in the room.

FOUR: When I am the only person of color in the room.

SEVEN: When I am the only person whose gender is in question in the room.

ELEVEN: When people call me "she" ...

NINE: When I have to choose between "male" and "female" on some document or application.

TEN: When there are no other options.

ELEVEN: When I am neither, or both, or something else entirely.

TEN: When my identity changes every single day and no one seems to understand that.

SIX: I feel the most naked when I am unexpectedly outed as transgender—not because I'm embarrassed about being trans, but because if rude and intrusive questions ensue, I suddenly feel obligated to be gracious and articulate and educate them.

FOURTEEN: I feel the most naked when someone tells me that I am beautiful

FOUR: and I find I cannot believe it.

ONE: I feel the most naked when I am falling asleep, or waking up.

THIRTEEN: There are fewer noises, my eyes are closed,

FIFTEEN: and all my vulnerabilities are able to come to the surface.

ONE:	Any walls or blocks I put up while awake completely fall away and I can no longer protect myself from how I really feel.
SEVEN:	I feel the most naked when I'm truly honest with myself.
FOUR:	And when I can truly be there for someone else,
EIGHT:	which happens only when I am able to be with myself first.
TWO:	When I am breathing new air.
TWELVE:	Clean air.
ELEVEN:	Fresh air.
FIVE:	Believing in myself again.
ONE:	Starting over.

(ensemble takes a breath together and says, in unison:)

ALL:	Naked.

(blackout)

VOICEOVER

GENDER
by Troy Osswold

Gender is something that seems simple, rather easy, when you're not looking at it too closely. Perhaps it is the people who do not know me, who in truth know me the best. The ones I walk by on the street, who sneak a second peak over the shoulder as soon as we've passed by each other. The ones with widened eyes and furrowed foreheads, their minds spinning in turmoil. Boy?! or Girl?! They cannot decide which word to use, what associations to make, whether they should be attracted or not – all as if knowing which one of the two was more visibly accurate underneath my clothes would cause instantaneous knowledge of my soul.

If you cannot look me in the eye, I will always remain a mystery.

DEAR PUSSY

by Anthony Neuman

I found you when I was just a child. I would play with you—in the bath, in my bed, on the couch, at church, and at school. I liked the way it felt to rub against you when I was on my belly, with my toes pressed into the floor, and my body rocking back and forth. When I would knead against you hard and fast it would make my whole body shake. I was told not to touch you when others were around. I was told you were private. I strayed down to your opening when I learned about sex. In and out, in and out—just like the movies showed me. Why didn't you like that? Everyone told me that you were supposed to like it.

When you bled, I hated you. I threw you away, and tried to ignore you. I hid you from the world, and myself. I would scour and scrub you for hours in the shower, desperately trying to make you clean again. You betrayed me. You became some sort of symbol of womanhood—and that was something that you knew I didn't want.

I kept you hidden under layers of clothes, rolled socks, or a condom full of hair gel (to get the perfect texture). Underneath this façade, you were the last thing the world would ever expect. I hid you from the naive women that fawned over my deft hands and insatiable mouth with zero knowledge or even care about your existence. They came for me with complete apathy for you. I didn't care about you either. Pleasure was something that you no longer deserved. Lack of release was your punishment.

Bound and castigated for years, finally a sweet release unexpectedly came along.

We shed our coverings for her. Strip down to absolute nakedness, like never before. You are exposed to her fervent eyes. Devoured before even being touched. She reaches for you. As I have trained you to respond, you start to withdraw, but this time something stops us. This time you want it. I can feel how you swell in her hand. Sopping wet, like usual. Embarrassingly messy. She marinates in it. Thirsts for it. This makes us comfortable with a vulnerability that is both virginal and instinctive. You surrender in full to her touch. Open wide like the vulnerable creature you have always denied being. You wrap yourself around her and there is an immediate sense of home. Suddenly alterations and specifications don't seem so important. Those deliberate distinctions of gender that feel for the first time, unnecessary. After years of striving for a confidence within comfort of self, we find it with her deep inside of you. Deep where it hurts. Deep where no one else has been. Unexplored territory, virgin flesh in her hands becomes an unexpected constant craving.

I no longer want to be rid of you. I don't want to cut you out. Have you removed. Gone. I would miss the chance to feel that sense of home with my lover inside of me. I don't want to take away that deeper intimacy now that I've found it.

COMING OUT... TWICE?

by AP Looze

It's always good if everyone's drunk *and* happy.

My sister's 21st birthday was quite the smash, so to speak. It was one of those restaurants where the food is way too good, we are way too loud, and the wine poured until I found myself sweating a lot and feeling particularly happy with the future—but it was in an unreasonable sort of way because I couldn't think of anything specific I was happy about. It's called drunk false hope. I get it a lot.

After my dad yells one final compliment to the waiter, we step out onto Madison's capitol square, where the air is sticky. A storm is brewing. We need to go about half way around the square before reaching the street my Aunt and Uncle live on and where we can catch a cab. During that walk, my aunt sidles up to me.

"Soooo, have you told them yet?"

All I can do is laugh.

***

Earlier that summer, I had gone to visit her and my uncle out in the Wisconsin boonies to "get away from it all" for a couple of days. While sitting around a camp fire, my aunt had asked me the same question, "have you told them yet?" I looked at her, totally puzzled. Told them *what*? *What* is it that she's talking about and who are *they*? And then it dawned on me. She's knows I'm gay? Wait...*she knows I'm gay?* And she's wondering if I've told my parents? I played stupid.

My aunt covered her mouth. "Am I not supposed to know?" she asked. "Your grandma and I have been wondering... *'I think that little granddaughter of mine is a lesbian'* she keeps telling me. I thought you would have told your parents by now...sorry for assuming. Maybe you're not gay!" And she threw her hands up in the air.

Do I look that gay? All this time I thought I'd been covering it up pretty well. I guess baggy shorts, white t's and bandanas are not things that heterosexual women typically wear. It made me wonder what the hell my high school boyfriends were thinking in dating me...

***

So, in the midst of my laughter, in the August night, I shake my head. I would be heading back to Minneapolis for school in less than a week and I still hadn't told my parents that...*haha*— I'd been dating women and...*haha*— sometimes I'd been fucking them in their house while they were asleep and...*haha* — about that one time on the kitchen counter and that other time in their bed when they were at work...

"Well," my aunt said, "you should probably tell them. They're cool folks; they won't freak out."

She and my uncle walk back to their apartment, and my family hails a cab back to our house. It has finally begun to rain. My sister, in her birthday drunken stupor, decides maybe it's best if she goes to bed. The rest of us decide on another round.

With a gin and tonic in my hands, I sit down across the room from my dad and his knob creek neat—his favorite and most dangerous drink—, each of us tucking our right leg under our left. My mom remains in the kitchen. I hear ice colliding with the sides of a metal shaker—dirty gin martini, three olives. It will take her a minute to join us, so dad starts to ramble on about how he's right about everything—a common thread in his often one-sided, drunken conversations.

Feeling saucy, and slightly intoxicated, I challenge him.

"Tell me something you're right about, then," I say, bringing the gin and tonic to my lips again.

He turns his head to face me, pauses with a contemplative glare, squints his eyes, bites his lower lip and turns his calculating gaze toward me. He then points a finger directly at me, and in a drawn out, confident, and conclusive drawl says,

"You're gay."

We hear footsteps from the kitchen, and in walks my mom, stirring her martini.

"Oh, did I miss it?"

In my head I'm like wait a minute, *how long have these folks known?* and as though he could hear my brain, my dad bursts out "oh, we've known since you were about...three. That's when we knew we had an interesting child on our hands."

And my mom says, "yeah, we didn't want to say anything when you started dating guys, hoping you'd figure it out...and you were always so fussy about dresses..."

Sitting there, finding myself in a buzzed combination of dumbfounded and smitten, all I can do is blush and sip my drink. Until my mom takes another sip of her martini, swallows, and totally in stride asks, "Are you thinking about transitioning?"

My mind goes blank for a split second. I feel sweat collecting on my brow. How do they go from me being gay to me being trans? The skirt I'm wearing suddenly doesn't fit so well. After my moment of panic, I simply, state, that "no, I'm not thinking about it," even though my insides are burning, wanting to scream out YES YES YES. YES I DO. YES I WANT MY TITS TO BE TAKEN OFF AND YES I WANT A DEEPER VOICE, AND WHEN I KISS YOU ON THE CHEEK GOOD BYE I WANT YOU TO FEEL MY WHISKERS.

"We just wanted to know," my dad says, "we support you no matter what."

***

14

Earlier that summer, my dad and I had had a couple of nights to ourselves. We got a six-pack of PBR and shot the shit for a few hours. One night, standing at the kitchen sink, watching a storm roll in over the back yard, we started talking about sports and how I was a good tennis player in high school. At one point I just randomly asked him if he'd ever wanted a boy.

He looked at me, tears in his eyes, and said: "I just wanted kids... I wanted to raise them to be whatever they wanted to be. That's the best gift I could ask for in the world."

MORE FUN THAN POOPING
by Jaime Hokanson

The conversation that would not shut up in my head for quite some time went like this:

omigod I'm trans
omigod I'm trans
omigod I'm trans
... am I trans?

One way I began to convince myself that yes, I was trans, was to start reading memoirs about gender. Since I'm on the transfeminine spectrum, the ones that resonate with me the most are written by trans women, and one such memoir was written by a 50-something year-old trans woman who said she knew she was a woman when she was only *3 years old*.

Here are some of the most profound things I knew when I was three years old:

Pooping is fun
Bert is the yellow one
Look! There is a kitty!

There's not much else in my mind before that.

Between the ages of hot wheels birthday presents and standing in the boys line in elementary school, however, I do have a few vague memories – especially of often being misgendered – as in my parents fielding the common exclamation: "what a beautiful daughter you have!"

Like most parents, mine couldn't just say, "thank you" and move on. And therefore I was conditioned, in a way, to feel embarrassed and angry whenever it happened. I was deemed a weirdo for myriad reasons, and I had longish but not really girly hair... so although this didn't happen on a regular basis, it happened frequently enough to have an impact.

But I wasn't only anxious about being called a girl. I also remember my first time being called "sir." I had just checked out a book from our elementary school's tiny library, when the librarian said,

"Thank you, sir!"

And I freaked out inside. I'm not a sir! I'm not old enough! I'm not responsible enough! I'm not... boy enough.

Although I didn't know it at the time.

Back then, I was afraid of someone mistaking me for a girl, because, well, I was a boy and that was that, according to the line I was supposed to stand in to go to art class; according to the team I had to play on at recess; according to the table I had to sit at in the cafeteria. Who knew that X number of years later, I'd occasionally be crossing my fingers that some people might see me as female out in the world...

I recently changed my name from a male-assigned one to one that's commonly used by people of all genders. When interacting with people in such a way that they have no other gender markers - like emailing someone I've never met - most people either assume I'm male or just make sure not to refer to me using gendered words or pronouns. I'm not trying to trick anyone. Personally, my name change was one way of specifically marking myself *outside* the gender binary.

EVLOUTION
by Jessica Englund

I don't know how to talk to you,
about you
I wish I knew how to tell you
that I also don't know how to feel,
about you

Tell me again, what you want?

You are not who I met.

...That beautiful woman standing by the bar
Sly smile enticing
You've perfected this technique I see
Effectively pulling my clit closer
Walk over to me as I stand alone
Request for liquor lingering in the air
You look at me like a lion hunts prey
One week later you accept my invitation
And fuck me like the butch you are
Late nights spent divulging all that we are
Confessions freely given and
Vulnerabilities traded for trust

Now,
Silence seeps from your pores
Stifling the love I use to fill each room
Days spent ignoring the search
For your identity
You hold my identify against me
Indirectly, sometimes. Perhaps.

You're right, I'm a women-loving woman
Long live the lesbian
and fuck yes for dyke culture!
Does this mean I should stop loving you?
Throw in the cards
and let you tell me how I feel?

I'll take it,
over your self-loathing stagnant immobility
Please stop pretending this will go away
if you will it.

I thought I had finally found
what I'd been waiting for...
Here she is, the soft butch of my dreams
Full of energy, passion and desire
But the more you struggle,
the farther I fall from you...

Who are you now?
Are you the woman I fell in love with?
Hiding in this venus fly trap
that has caught you?
(Gender purgatory, I like to call it...)
Or are you my quickly evolving boifriend
that I do not yet understand?
More than me wanting to be with you,
I don't want you to be with another woman.

Am I selfish?
Yes.
  Maybe.
        I don't know.
Am I angry?
Yes.
  Maybe.
        I don't know.

Do I miss you?
The *you* I first knew?
Yes. Of course.
I miss you,
and I will always miss the *you* that I fell in love with.

Instinct tells me to apologize for that.
But people apologize all too much and all too often.
No thanks.
I am not sorry.

THE STORY OF BOB

by Ben Resman

"It turned purple on me, dude! It turned purple on me!"

This is what I was shouting as they wheeled me quickly past my friend, who was standing in the hospital hallway, mouth open, holding an iced coffee. He'd been gone less than an hour. An hour ago everything was fine. This was the night before my forty-fourth birthday and I had a clot in my groin that was cutting off the blood supply to my new penis.

Twelve days prior, I'd taken a gamble. I was betting on the fact that I would have a good outcome—after all, I'd done my research—the three guys who'd had this done prior to me had fabulous dicks with very few complications. I rolled the dice and took what I thought was my best shot at having a sensate penis for the first time in my life. A penis I could stand up and pee through. A penis I could use to write my name in the snow. A penis I could play with. A penis someone else could play with. A penis that could slide inside another person. A penis that I could do the helicopter with. Was it painful? Yes. Swinging my legs out of bed for the first time made me pass out. Did it leave a huge and permanent scar on my forearm, my upper thigh and down my calf, where they'd harvested all that vein and tissue? Yes. Was it worth it?

Well, the day after the surgery, they wheeled me down to a bubbling hydrotherapy tank, where I was carefully undressed by three nurses, two hot blond Nordic glamazons and a handsome gay male nurse, whose comment as they lowered me into the tank was "well, that's certainly nothing to be ashamed of!" Was it worth it? Yes. And the moments that followed were worth it. Seeing my body in the water, my groin looking the way I'd always seen it in my head- no more phantom penis- this one was real and it was mine. I tried not to fall asleep in the water. I didn't want to miss watching it bob up and down in the bubbles for the first time. I remember thinking that would be a good name for him, on the occasion of his first baptism. Bob.

Five days later, Bob got an infection. The doctors weren't "too concerned", they said, "this isn't unusual for reconstructive surgery, let's see if we can get it under control. You should be able to leave the ICU as early as next week." By the next week, they were not so optimistic. They decided to go in surgically to treat the source of the infection. The night before my second surgery, I felt a weird pain my groin. I looked underneath my gown to see that Bob had suddenly turned dark purple.

They pumped me full of drugs and prepped me for emergency surgery. I remember one of the nurses asking the surgeon if she could 'take pictures to use as a teaching tool'. I was too drugged to refuse and started to cry as she snapped pictures of my dying cock. "Don't worry," she said, "the surgeons are very good. They'll save it." I was kept unconscious for the next two days, unaware that I'd had two more surgeries. I awoke on my birthday to the news that they'd been unable to save my penis. The surgeon, visiting me late that night said, "We can always try again with the other arm." My only thoughts were, "My God, what does my groin look like now? I'm grotesque, mangled, deformed. Will I ever be able to pee without being strapped to a catheter bag? Does this mean that I will NEVER have another orgasm?" My body looked like it had been run over by a lawnmower and I had nothing to show for it.

Even though they should not have released me, after 19 days in the ICU, I was hell-bent on getting out of there. I wanted to go home and never come back. This plan presented its own problems. It never occurred to me that once I got home, I wouldn't be able to find a doctor to treat me.

I couldn't bring myself to go back to the hospital that had performed the operation. My own doctor agreed to do wound treatment and staple pulling, but I shook violently whenever she touched me. Every urologist I called refused to book an appointment with me once they knew about my situation. I finally found one who agreed to remove my catheter, but only after weeks of hoop-jumping and a series of phone calls to 'a - guy-who-knew-a guy-who-maybe-used-to-work-with-trannies'. Of course, he asked if he could bring in medical students to observe, but I knew that it was not just to learn how to pull a catheter. I tried my best to answer questions and make it a Teachable Tranny Moment, despite feeling like a sideshow freak. The only question I got after they'd finally pulled the catheter out was "they're not going to LEAVE you like that, are they!?"

Physically weak and depleted, my self esteem began to circle the toilet. I contacted a friend who told me that maybe I should feel lucky. He knew a nurse on the reconstructive unit where I'd had my surgery. He said I should feel lucky because even though I was carrying some seriously fucked up junk in my jockeys, the guy who had his procedure after me needed 14 additional surgeries. The guy after him? Died.

That knocked the wind out of me. Died? A guy died having THIS surgery.

Maybe my friend was right. I should feel lucky. But at that moment all I could feel was sad. Then I thought, OK, I need to post something to the listserv I'd been on for years, tell my story, write about taking the risks seriously and talk to other guys whose surgeries had also failed. Get some advice about how to navigate this. I put in a post and waited. I got a few 'sorry to hear that, dude.' replies and then silence. Just silence. No one responded. It was only then that I realized that the guys whose surgeries fail don't post their results to listservs.

On the upside, I had friends to check on me, send me encouraging notes, bring me movies, books, cashew chicken salad and yes, adult diapers when my wound drainage started rising to flood level. I was also fortunate enough to have friends who are aware that wounds heal considerably faster when treated with generous amounts of marijuana. And I'm still alive, which is good news for me. And hopefully, it's also good news for the woman I met several months after all of this hell, and quickly fell in love with...

But that's a story for another time.

QUEER CONFESSIONS
by Alyx J. Hanson

I've been thinking a lot, lately, about gender (a logical result of the recent entrances of several lovely trans people into my life over the past year). I came to the realization that, ultimately, I identify as agendered — parts of me are feminine, parts quite decidedly masculine, and gender feels like something I put on and perform rather than something I ever really am.

As a consequence of all of this gender-related pondering, I found I wanted to step out and embrace the more masculine parts of myself in ways I had been too afraid to attempt before. And so, I made my first tentative forays into the men's department. It started with jeans — I wanted pants with actual fucking pockets. Then I bought a tie, because I liked the idea of ties and was fairly certain that I would look incredibly handsome if I started wearing them. The tie was followed by a second tie, and then a vest, and then another tie, and a few button-downs, and another tie...and soon, I found myself wearing men's clothing almost exclusively. I also started binding. Button-downs and vests and ties became a trademark look, rather than something I wore just to dress up.

And the strangest thing happened. The more I wore men's clothes, the more comfortable I became with the idea of being a girl. I still feel more or less genderless, but I am much more all right with playing "girl" and being read as cisgendered when I can look, at least in my eyes and the eyes of my boifriend, like the handsome young gentleman that I am in my head.

I am also queer, whatever the fuck that means.

I think that people are beautiful, wonderful, complex beings who deserve more freedom than what is given them by a label-crazy world. I am not exclusively attracted to men, so I am not straight. I am not exclusively attracted to women, so I am not a lesbian. But I am also not exclusively attracted to individuals who fall into the binary system of "male" or "female," and so I am not bisexual. I fall in love with people, not genders or body parts.

Sometimes, I put on heels and swivel my hips when I walk. I let my voice soften and slide it up half an octave, or drop it down a little and let it grow smooth and hypnotic. I rarely go so far as to put on a skirt or wear makeup or shave my legs, but still, some days, I am definitely a girl. I wield my femininity with the nearest approximation of finesse and grace I can muster. I wink and I flirt. I claim every curve and generally feel sexy.

Other days, my gender is less easily defined. I feel like a stud, walk with a swagger, and take up more space. I am strong and protective, working hard to make the people I love feel safe. I am masculine.

Most days, I find myself somewhere in between. Gender is something that I live, but it is not often something that I am. I put on gender like a sweater when I get up in the morning. I let it cover me, protect me, be the thing that people see when they look at me. But I never become the sweater. It never grows into a part of me. It always remains something external. Gender is something that I play at, like a child playing dress-up in hir parents' clothes—ze can wear the clothes in a reasonable facsimile of a real outfit, but they never quite fit like they're supposed to.

I am equally content being branded as she, he, ze, they; her, him, hir or them. You may refer to me by whatever pronouns you prefer. I embrace queer as a label because it is the one word I have found that encompasses all of who I am.

Non-conforming.
Boi.
Girl.
Beautiful.
Handsome.
Butch.
Femme.
Other.
Queer.

DEAR DAD
by Ethan Turcotte

(Two men on stage: one older, one younger. Young man is speaking to older man, but older man is doing his own thing - seeming to not see or hear young man. Older man could be fixing yard power tool, reading a book. Young man watches older man thoughtfully for a few seconds, then addresses the audience)

I don't do it very often, but tonight I decided to shave my face with a razor. Most of the time, I use small clippers to keep a sort of permanent scruff. There are a few reasons for this, but the one that is most important is that I have a lot of anxiety about people misreading my gender. I know that it's rarely an issue these days, that I can shave my face clean and people will still read me as male. But there's something about going through that experience of being misread that makes you die a little inside; you do anything you can not to feel that way again.

I guess I didn't give it much thought, just set up the usual accessories and grabbed a hand mirror. It had been a few months since shaving clean, and I was surprised at how much easier it was with a new razor. This act was fairly monotonous until I began to remember - you didn't raise me as a boy. You never taught me how to shave and as awkward and silly as it may have been, you never offered to teach me once I needed to. I pressed my tongue into my lower lip the way I watched you do it when I was a little girl, not realizing then why I was so entranced. But I remember that move all these years later - it makes it so much easier to get at the space below my lip. Standing in the shower, I became overwhelmed. I felt a mix of things all at once; anger at an early life missed out on, loss of a possible way to connect with you, and still happy that I'm me – a guy of my own design. I had to learn how to shave by trial and error. Watching and feeling the way my hair grows, twisting and turning the razor to meet it head-on. I got cut up a lot in the beginning, but I was learning how to navigate my body with its changes.

There's a certain strength in that; I am exactly who I want to be. But in creating this body and life of my own choosing, I've had to teach myself things you were never able to. Being self-taught in subjects as ancient as life itself, missing the bonding of a father and son, these things take their toll in other ways. How do I interact with other men? What are the social cues I should follow now? I trip over my awkward male self as my physical appearance changes faster than my social skills. The mistakes I make now are profound yet have no connection to history. They're not as insignificant as the shaving cuts on my face.

What do you think of me now? I still don't know. Do you still see that blond haired, big blue-eyed little girl who clung to your every move? The kid who dropped the matchbox cars when you popped your head in the room to ask if she wanted to come to the hardware store with you? At 12, I hated you, because I wasn't turning into you. We went through a difficult ten years after that. You let me down in some way that I couldn't describe then and is hard for me to articulate even now. You changed around me once my body began resembling a woman and I acted out to show my devastation at your rejection of the real me. You stopped treating me like the boy I really was. Neither one of us could see it, and we treated each other like shit. Did we do irreparable damage?

I'd like to think you'd be proud of me now, proud of the person I've become. I'm very much like you in a lot of ways. I wish we had both realized the boy I was at the time, because our relationship could be very different now. Maybe I wouldn't have so many cuts on my face.

CONGRUITY

by Erica Fields

(Spotlight on Erica — she is a middle-aged, transgender woman.)

Congruity.

This is a new term in my personal lexicon. I have been using it to describe how I feel about my new body and its connection to my being. It is a word that has that intellectual appeal as it describes what is so base. I am now whole.

Whole? *What does that even mean?*

I'm not sure. I just know that as I walk through life now I feel complete. It isn't something that has visibly changed, except to me and my Doctor, or perhaps someday my lover. That is not the point. It has affected everything I do. I now have a real feeling of inner happiness.

In my past there had always been a sense of anxiousness as I did everything. I was quite good at masking it with wit and charm but it was always there. I couldn't walk down the street or through a crowd without this deep feeling of discomfort. Like I was going to spill someone's drink as I clumsily bumped into them. That feeling was constant. I just accepted it as a character flaw or some psychological quirk in me. I was constantly incongruous.

Now I have lost that sense. I suddenly noticed it the other night at dinner. I was walking to the bathroom, through tight tables filled with diners. I negotiated the path to the bathroom without any sense of nervousness. Not once did I feel that I was about to knock over a tray of food or trip on the leg of a chair. I surprised myself. I think this was just one more realization of the depth of my gender identity issue. It felt good to have resolved something I had never thought was resolvable. Something that I had never connected with my underlying sense of gender. And to think that it was just about having congruity...

As I lay awake that Sunday night before surgery, I had expected to have a revelation about the change that was about to happen – about the attendant differences from that old plumbing.

I didn't.

Instead, there has been this sense of normality. As if *this* was how it always should have been. A familiarity, if you like, with something that should be unfamiliar.

I had an actor friend recently tell me that she had always sensed that there was something missing whenever I did scenes, and now that I am myself there is a connection that was not there before.

Congruity.

That is what it is... and a peace of mind that I have never felt before.

HOW TO MAKE LOVE TO A TRANS PERSON
by Gabe Moses

Forget the images you've learned to attach
To words like *cock* and *clit*,
Chest and *breasts*.

Break those words open
Like a paramedic cracking ribs
To pump blood through a failing heart.

Push your hands inside.
Get them messy.
Scratch new definitions on the bones.
Get rid of the old words altogether.
Make up new words.
Call it a *click* or a *ditto*.

Call it the sound he makes
When you brush your hand against it
through his jeans,
When you can hear his heart
knocking on the back of his teeth
And every cell in his body is breathing.

Make the arch of her back a language
Name the hollows of each of her vertebrae
When they catch pools of sweat
Like rainwater in a row of paper cups
Align your teeth with this alphabet of her spine
So every word is weighted with the salt of her.

When you peel layers of clothing from his skin
Do not act as though you are
changing dressings on a trauma patient
Even though it's highly likely that you are.

Do not ask if she's "had the surgery."
Do not tell him that the needlepoint bruises

on his thighs look like they hurt.
If you are being offered a body
That has already been laid upon an altar of surgical steel
A sacrifice to whatever gods govern bodies
That come with some assembly required
Whatever you do,
Do not say that the carefully sculpted landscape
Bordered by rocky ridges of scar tissue
Looks almost natural.

If she offers you breastbone
Aching to carve soft fruit from its branches
Though there may be more tissue in the lining of her bra
Than the flesh that rises to meet it,
Let her ripen in your hands.
Imagine if she'd lost those swells to cancer,
Diabetes,
A car accident instead of an accident of genetics
Would you think of her as less a woman then?
Then think of her as no less one now.

If he offers you a thumb-sized sprout of muscle
Reaching toward you when you kiss him
Like it wants to go deep enough inside you
To scratch his name on the bottom of your heart
Hold it as if it can-
In your hand, in your mouth
Inside the nest of your pelvic bones.
Though his skin may hardly do more than brush yours,
You will feel him deeper than you think.

Realize that bodies are only a fraction of who we are
They're just oddly-shaped vessels for hearts
And honestly, they can barely contain us
We strain at their seams with every breath we take
We are all pulse and sweat,
Tissue and nerve ending
We are programmed to grope and fumble until we get it right.
Bodies have been learning each other forever.
It's what bodies do.
They are grab bags of parts
And half the fun is figuring out

All the different ways we can fit them together;
All the different uses for hipbones and hands,
Tongues and teeth;
All the ways to car-crash our bodies beautiful.
But we could never forget how to use our hearts
Even if we tried.

That's the important part.

Don't worry about the bodies.
They've got this.

SUPERHERO
by Ethan Lyn Draeger

I am a superhero when I have a good influence on the way children see and understand gender. When they matter-of-factly state that I'm half boy. When they ask about my gender and I tell them it's okay. When I gently, at first, and then later, with more feeling, remind them that a boy monster can wear his hair any way he likes. When a girl comes to school with a super short haircut and the other kids make fun of her and say "she looks like a boy", I can walk over with all of my authority and tell her she looks fabulous, and I love the new cut. I am a superhero when the non-conforming girl comes to me with a cut on her ankle, and I know the only Band-Aids left are Disney Princess ones. We search together through the first-aid box, find the gauze and medical tape, and find a good alternative out of the tools we've been given.

WOUNDED
by *Davey Ethan Wilkes*

I am the heir to a fortune of misfortunes,
birthed from the broken-open loins of drag queens
who've been dead for decades.

I was made from a rich history of small triumphs and a host of
just-missed victories,
built from the spilt blood of butches, dykes, bull daggers,
femmes, faggots, fairies, queers and queens. What I mean is:

this has *always* been about gender.

Which is why I will not be disinherited,
told my transition takes me out of the communities
that birthed me to begin with.

This is what I offer:
I will claim you, if you will claim me.
Not just my past,
as a butch dyke, born into female labels unwillingly,
but me in my entirety, which means
male, man, masculine, FTM;
it's who I am,
and it doesn't give me any less claim to this legacy
of gay community
or identity.

Beyond fearsome femmes and passing transmen,
before the riots at the Stonewall Inn,
and everything since then:
I will claim you, if you will claim me.

Lesbian separatists, andro-dykes, straight men givin' guys
head on the weekends, michfest faithful's, cross dressers, bi,
tri, omni, pomo, metro, just-not-quite-hetero-sexuals, straight
kids of gay folks, 18th century secret lovers, allies, closet cases
and sexworkers, World War vets who were in it for the men,
transwomen, genderqueers, 3-beer queers,

and bend-over boyfriends:
I will claim you, if you will claim me.

This will not be easy.

Homophobia created our communities.
As a result we are always on the offensive,
usually taking aim at each other;
resistance is as much a part of this identity
as fucking outside the lines of polite sexuality.

If you can't remember what to resist, pick up your local paper.
The New York Times asks, "Is lesbianism dead?"
It's an article about transmen.
I don't know who should be more hurt by this,
me or the women they're calling extinct.
Go down to your neighborhood community center;
gay men still can't give blood
because they are all carriers of disease.
Turn on the TV; we are just comic relief.

We have made too many dirty deals behind each other's backs
to be taken seriously.
So, let's get it all out in the open,
put motion into a movement based on something more
than just a common enemy:
I will bear witness for you, if you will bear witness for me.

We need each other.

We will never not need each other.
Whether we do it out of fear, or love, or lust, or distrust,
we need to keep each other
closer
because we aren't getting anywhere alone
because we still walk with shame
because we are being identified more by what we wear than
who we love or fuck or trust
because you should never turn your back on people who've
learned to conceal switchblades in the slits of their wrists.

Because we wound each other.

Because we've never had to face who we've left behind
look them in the eye, and try to say it was worth it,
because we neglect the memories
of the people who've died for this
because far from being over this battle is still bloody
because equal rights are not inevitable,
but having to fight for them is,
because we're running out of spaces in the sand
to draw lines in.

We are overlapped.

I cannot find the line where one history ends
and the next begins.
We owe it to out lineage to claim each other,
to make payments on our common debt
to those whose blood has dried and flaked from the fences,
sidewalks, and cells
they were slaughtered in,
to the first person who said "gay"
with a knowing smile and a wink,
to the first person who had "queer"
wielded at them as a weapon,
took it from their assailant, shielded themselves and said
they were home.
I call you home.

Call me home.

ACT TWO

BISCUITS
by Lane McKiernan, scripted by Anthony Neuman

(Three FTMs on the couch. Voice over of an instructional video on how to tie a tie is heard while the boys are fumbling with their ties for a while before Sandy enters — video is not seen, only heard.)

SANDY: Frank, honey, are you trying to get rid of me? You're not thinking of replacing me with the man in that god awful tie, are you?

FRANK: Of course not. Just since it's boy's night I didn't want to impose on your precious time, and you know these fellas don't have pretty ladies to tie their ties, and I was just trying to help them out so we could all look real good when we go out *(she can cut him off at any time here, walk around the couch, plant herself in his lap and kiss him — the other boys blush)*

SANDY: Dinner is almost ready. Now y'all set the table and get ready. We've got to get you out on the town.

BOYS: Yes ma'am.

(They are up and to their duties. FRANK helps SANDY in the kitchen while JIM and BUDDY set the table and all the boys get dressed. Dinner is placed on the table — Big platters of it. Chicken cooked in onions and tomatoes, black-eyed peas and greens, and a whole plate of buttermilk biscuits two inches high. They sit and eat. BUDDY specifically is engrossed in the meal, ignoring the conversation.)

JIM: Sandy, this all looks so good. When did you learn to cook?

SANDY: When I was a little girl. Wasn't so much learning as it was watching and repeating. Where are you going for boy's night?

FRANK: The 19 bar for pool night. I think Jim here is lookin' to beat me for once.

JIM: Nope, I've given up on that, but I'm hoping if we play teams we might have a shot against Frank.

SANDY: Well, he's just showing off the moves I taught him. Frank and I used to go to Bar 19 all the time when we first started seeing each other. I think I impressed him with some of my pool shark moves.

FRANK: Pretty sure we impressed each other, sweetheart.

SANDY: You always were a great shot.

JIM: *(quick subject change)* These biscuits are just delicious-

(SANDY starts watching BUDDY eat.)

SANDY: Why thank you. *(Pause)* Frank, why didn't you tell me this one was from the South? I would have cooked this kind of food weeks ago. Where do you call home, honey?

(BUDDY looks up from his plate for the first time, pauses to chew and swallow.)

BUDDY: The Ozarks.

SANDY: Uh huh. South enough for black-eyed peas to taste like home but far enough West that the accent gets all blurry. You get homesick, you just let me know. I've always got the fixings for peas and greens, biscuits and sausage gravy.

BUDDY: Yes ma'am.

SANDY: Now you be sure to be careful out on boy's night-
           there's one thing ya'll don't understand. Girls
           don't know that it's *boy's* night.

BUDDY: Yes ma'am.

SANDY: Enough of the ma'am, honey. You're family.

BUDDY: *(to audience)* Finally, I understand why I always
           feel just a little homesick at meals here in
           Minnesota, even if it is the best place I've ever
           lived. Where I come from, people like us, with
           our short hair and bound chests and men's
           clothes have a hard enough time getting in the
           door with the families that raised us as girls,
           much less invited to the table.

FRANK: Nobody in *my* family ever cooked this good,
           thank goodness I've got Sandy here to feed me,
           or I'd be eating TV dinners every night.

BUDDY: *(still to the audience)* But here, where it is a little
           easier, a little safer to be me, the food is all so
           pale and bland. I miss the flavors that feel like
           home and the way that sharing them with people
           you care about is more sacred than the prayer I
           was raised to say before I ate. *(He takes a
           moment before rejoining the scene.)*

JIM: But what about me? What if I get homesick?

FRANK: You let me know and we'll go right down to
           Ingebretsen's and get you some lefse? Pass the
           chicken.

BUDDY: With a side of lutefisk! Pass the biscuits.

(Laughter, and some time to finish eating)

SANDY: Well you boys better be getting on to boy's night-
           remember what I told you.

39

FRANK: Please Darlin, let us help you clean up.

SANDY: Always a gentleman that man of mine. *(She is shooing them up and out toward the door. They stand, backs against the wall. She ties their ties, JIM first, then BUDDY, then FRANK.)* There were two things my mama made sure I knew how to do right before she let me leave home: make biscuits and tie a man's tie. And something tells me you don't want me to forget how to do either one. *(She takes a moment to look them over.)* Alright boys ya'll go have yourselves a good time.

(Blackout)

VOICEOVER

FOR YOU
by Rebecca Lawrence

For you, I promise never to ask if you're sure.
For you, I promise never to ask
if you have really thought this through.
For you, I promise to not look at you like others do,
when they ask those questions
Because I have laid beside you for weeks of sleepless nights
Knowing that those questions repeat in your head,
without rest.
For you, I promise never to question your resolve
Because I know you do, every day.
For you, I promise never to ask if you are really sure
Because even if you can't confidently answer "yes"
At least I know you can finally sleep through the night.

MINE TO FACE

by Katie Burgess

(Two chairs are set up side-by-side center stage. Katie, a young transgender woman, sits on one. She is on a bus.)

I woke up. Not sure if it was the diesel engine of the Greyhound bus or my own snoring that did it, I proceeded to try and casually wipe the drool off my face.

His nose was about six inches away from my cheek, his eyes slanted against the early morning sunlight streaming in through the oversized emergency exit windows, lighting up what he was so intently peering at: my face. My naked face – greasy, crease lines where my sweatshirt had dug into my cheek, covered with stubble.

"What the fuck are you?"

He got the attention of the row in front of us with that one. They were curious too.

The more I pushed him away and told him to back up, sit down, mind your own damn business, the more everyone else on the bus got interested. Everyone was asking questions. Everyone wanted to know. Even the bus driver occasionally took moments to glance up at me in the mirror.

That damned reflection. The daily betrayal.

I thought that I would have had at least another hour. My digital watch alarm was even set for it. I knew exactly where my razor was. And the piss graffitied shit bucket bus bathroom was only five feet away from me. Five feet covered with a busload of dangerously inquisitive stares and one raging asshole. I hadn't been eager to discover what I would find in that little portapotty mirror. And now I had run out of time. It had found me.

And it wasn't the first time.

This reflection has followed me like a ghost my whole life. What do you want? Why won't you leave me in peace?

When I was younger, acting in high school plays, I would avoid the green room by all means. As much as catching a glimpse of myself, anxiously lingering in one of those infinite mirrors and I would break my character. There was no more pretending. I was forced to face the reality that my stage makeup was amateur, my costume gaudy, my physical proportions were nothing like Shakespeare intended. My cursorily grown beard disgraced the royal prestige of *Macbeth*'s court. I would never convince anyone with this sophomoric rouse.

The effect translated into my non-stage life as well. So often, simply passing by dark windows, opening glass doors, washing my hands in the bathroom, would cause some part of me to break. My character would be ruined. The show would be a flop. You'd laugh me off stage.

Every morning, I – we – would lose our self together in the bathroom. Mostly I would obsess over my hair. Other days I would just stare-toothbrush half out of my mouth-directly into my own eyes. I was fascinated by the ways that I could move my head side to side and my eyes would seemingly stay in place, watching back, like they weren't even my own. My eyes would watch my eyes would watch my eyes would watch my eyes until I couldn't stand it anymore, or, more likely, my brother couldn't stand it anymore and kicked me out. I'd wash the dried toothpaste away from my lips and pretend to start my day.

After leaving my mother's apartment, I found myself staring into bathroom mirrors in the same way on those unlucky occasions of being overdrugged on hallucinogenics and unfortunately needing to retreat to a bathroom for any number of reasons. It was often a psychological desert – my thirst for sanity steadily growing with every step further into my reflection. My eyes locked on my eyes as wave after wave of penetrating drug induced psychosis washed over what should have been, what once was, what never could be, my face. My face – even the words lost meaning in my mouth. I would stumble out of the bathroom asking my drugged up cohort what happened to my face. Where was my face? I've lost my face. It was a running gag after a while. If anyone had overthrown their limit on whatever drug we were consuming en masse, they would exclaim, "I've lost my face."

Drug humor.

Today this ghost has turned flesh and sits comfortably cramped into the bus seat next to mine. Cozy and intimate as ever. "What the fuck are you?" The words hang in the air like so much exhaust hangs behind this bus machine we ride through the infinite mass of Midwest corn fields. Finally one man stands up above the sea of angry faces and faces mine. "Everybody sit down, shut up, and mind your own business."

I had helped him roll a joint several stops ago. He was struggling with his dried out stash and he knew I was good from the cigarettes that I had been rolling at each of the previous stops. We didn't say our names. There was no hands shook. I just took the paper and showed him. Hello.

He was the only one standing. So I stood up too. Everybody was finally quiet. I walked the five foot gauntlet to the back of the bus and closed the door behind me. Lavatory Occupied. It was time to make peace with this ghost.

I know exactly what the fuck I am.

And this is my face.

This is mine to face.

BOY OR GIRL?

by Ethan Lyn Draeger

We're in the hallway at school, and their line is unusually impressive. As we turn a corner by the library, Eh Loh, an eager seven-year-old asks me: "Are you a boy or a girl?"

(sigh)

I respond: "Some people think I'm a girl, and some people think I'm a boy. What do you think?"

Not missing a beat, he informs me: "I think you're a boy."

When I ask why, he tells me: "Because you wear boy clothes, and you have a mohawk."

"That's okay!" I tell him, and inside I am ecstatic that he can see who I really am.

TWO WEEKS LATER - It's snacktime and I'm out of the room looking for the marker bin that's never in the same place twice. Eh Loh is looking for me. He wants to talk to me and asks my coworker:

"Where'd that other dude go? Where'd he go?"

You would have thought the kid had punched someone in the nose.

My coworker reels, and fires back, in my assumed defense:

"You mean SHE? I'm pretty sure HER parents wouldn't have named her BETHANY if she was a BOY!"

I hear the encounter second-hand, in the computer lab, where I don't have space to react. I can only imagine Eh Loh's reaction. I'm afraid that he will think I made fun of him. That he'll be embarrassed about thinking I was a boy. I'm afraid he'll think that I lied, and that I'm really a girl.

ONE WEEK LATER - It's snack time again. Eh Loh walks over to me and stares up into my face.

"Are you a boy or a girl?" he asks, as though we've never discussed this before.

"What do you think?" I inquire again.

"I think you're a boy. *(pause)* And half girl."

(sigh)

Everything is going to be fine.

PINK AND BLUE: A (SHORT) LOVE STORY
by Andrea Jenkins

(Two women on stage — one transgender, one cisgender.)

She loves me, she loves me- not!

That's what I kept telling myself each night after dining with her. It's been seven months and we still haven't kissed; sure there have been lingering hugs that feel really good- and glancing smiles that melt my heart.

She loves me, she loves me not.

I have time, and she – has no freedom. Our choices are dictated by the forces of our artificial environments - busyness for the sake of being busy; and then there is art, creation, culture. But even more than that, our choices are shaped by the societal norms that have been so deeply embedded in the trenches like journalists in the War on Terror, that we don't even recognize them. Only the Shock and Awe is real; those damn people with their mouthy ideologies, snap judgments and those stares, that bore right through you. "Can you believe she's with him, (uh, I mean her) - what's up with that?"

I want to tell her it's okay to love me - I want to say let go and follow your heart's desire. I want to say we can be the new Modern Family (Post Modern) even. But - I don't say that. And each time I give up and think to myself this can never work out, she calls and that dusky voice says, "I've got a couple hours on Thursday evening..." and I'm all caught up in it again.

She loves me. I think she's attracted to my masculinity. Or is it my femininity? Or is it the dual nature of my identity that is drawing her in? Is it the fact that I can offer up adventure just by being? Her mind is sharp and bright, she loves food from different cultures and art in multiple genres - not that different from me in that aspect. She is a dancer in a symbolic choreography that suggests, "I am open to all the universe has to offer."

She loves me not. I think I am attracted to her interior life- the side that few are privileged to witness - the life that is bound up with constrictions, ropes and restraints. I am attracted to the part of her soul that wants to be controlled - to a point - and only after consent. I think I am attracted to that part that wants more. More sensuality, more carnality, more abundance, more love.

She loves, she loves me not. That's what I keep telling myself each time I want to reach out and take her hand and hold it in mine, and look into her tiny eyes and say the words that want to come out but don't. The words that would inform her about the complexity of my life; a life that has been shaped in a restrictive society that forced me to be someone that was not me. A life of being female while living in a male body.

People are willing to accept the fact that I have successfully made the transitional journey from male to female - in fact many are in awe of this, they call me things like "Brave, Confident, Courageous". What they are not willing to understand is that I am still attracted to beautiful. And yet I am hesitant to place her hand in my hand and to look into those tiny eyes and say those words.

She loves me, but not really. Maybe she is in love with that which I represent and I - I am in love with her - really? Don't get me wrong, it would be nice to find someone who is willing to take a chance with me, perhaps samba with me, and be willing to take a stance for me. Yes, that would be nice. It has been said that teamwork requires trust, a willingness to believe that your partner has your back - and is ready to fight to salvage the only (true) love they have ever known.

The last time we drank Riesling from plastic cups - there were two cups, one pink and one blue (well actually it was pretty dark and we really couldn't tell which was which) but there was a choice to be made to made - and we sat in the Sculpture Garden and she chose blue.

"Does it matter?"

"Yes."

"Why?"

"Because it's always the little things that really matter," I said.

Small gestures have a way of sending signals. Yet in our politeness we often miss them. Sometimes it's just a look that can express so much more than words. How long have I waited, waited just to hold you, wrap my love around you; to say "I love you" to someone who does not have my blood running through their veins? And then I see that look, that laughs and weeps, the look that longs for connection with another soul - that look that seeks direction, protection; and what I fear most is - rejection.

She loves me?

She loves me not?

FRIDAY SUPPLIES
by TJ Kampa

In the still silence
of the bathroom sit
the tools of my transformation.
Alcohol wipes, band-aids, syringes
and a prescribed holy vial
wait to be called to duty.
Excitement, apprehension,
anticipation, fear as I sit
looking at my thigh for a target.
The viscous liquid creeps
toward the correct dose.
Tiny beads of sweat collect
on the back of my neck as
I ready myself for what's ahead.
Breathe, relax, inject
delivering hormones
to make me feel complete.
The hair grows, the voice drops,
I'm on my way.

TRANS.SEXUAL.ALITY
by J.L. Mohnkern

My community is my home, my safe space,
my realm of empowerment, my passion.
Until someone addresses me with a label,
an incorrect assumption,
and "home" is suddenly less safe. Less mine.

She reads my lipstick as *lesbian,*
My skirt as an invitation that
I'm looking for my butch.
My body as a place to be put within the binary
that they are all trying so hard to break.
So happy to find out that I am not *straight*
I am not *just* an *ally*
that I am *part* of them
that she never bothers to find out
what I am or *who* I am.

He reads me as *straight,*
My lipstick as an invitation,
My skirt as a demand,
My body as something that must be his,
that must be ready for him and wanting him.
He catcalls, gropes, grabs for the attention
he feels he deserves.
Because I must fit within his comfort zone.

The outside world is where I live in stealth
like Peter Parker you'd never know my clothes
are covering up another layer unless you asked.

Bisexuality was my home, until I moved -
because I found there was more to me
than what would fit within the confines of their walls.

I realized that *bi* was an inaccurate and perhaps insulting label
to attempt to claim who or what

I was drawn to or fell for.
To claim that I was attracted to
two sexes, two genders
was limiting, and insulting to the
beautiful gender spectrum held out before me.
The beautiful bodies that refused to be placed
within the *male* or *female* boxes.
The beautiful minds that were both and neither
all at the same time.

So what am I then?

I am not gay or lesbian or bi or trans.
I am not a tranny chaser.
I am not straight.
I am not any label proclaimed for me.
I am not a femme looking for a butch.
I am not a bi trying to have it all.
I am simply trying to find my place
in my community,
fearful that there is nothing for me here.

JUST ME
by Kelly Waterman

When I was little, I didn't have any sense of Gender. Although I was considered a "tomboy", I never really felt like one. I was just being me. Sure I was a girl, but if I played football and climbed trees, did that make me a "tomBOY"? Or did it just make me a girl who liked to play football and climb trees? I didn't understand that if you wanted to play football you had to have a penis and if you wanted to play with dolls you had to have a vagina, and that if your genitals did not match a particular activity then there must be something wrong.

One day in the middle of 3rd grade, I decided to go outside and play. It was hot, so I took my shirt off. A neighbor boy was riding his bike nearby, and then stopped, got off his bike and told me to put my shirt on because I was a girl. Up until then I didn't know if I was a boy or a girl, so when it was made known to me that indeed I was a girl, I was in a bit of a shock. Not only was my Gender revealed, but I learned that people of my Gender could not take their shirts off on public.

From that moment on my Gender or Gender Presentation became an issue of which I have spent a life time dealing with. The battles about clothing began. Dolls that I never wanted were received as gifts, and I had to ride a "girls" bike, which mortified me.

In Grade School, my best friend was a boy named Tom and we did everything together. We rode our bikes, played football and climbed trees. By 5th grade I could beat anybody in any sport. I ruff housed with the boys, and I teased the girls. It was great!

My teachers, however, did not share in my joy. Meetings were had and observations were made. I was pulled out of class to have conversations about Gender with the School Psychologist. In Middle School, I was forced to take Ritalin because I couldn't "sit still". None of the boys could "sit still" either, but I never saw them in the Nurse's Office taking a pill like I had to. I remained socially awkward and did not fit in with either the boys or the girls throughout my entire youth and adolescence. It was a lonely time.

Now I am all grown up and my Gender Presentation has taken many twists and turns. I can't even remember the last time I bought an article of clothing from the Women's side if the store. I have connected more and more to the Queer community and my internalized sense of shame and wrongness has faded. I have experienced acceptance, peace and inner pride in regards to by Gender and my masculinity.

In 2005, before my mother died of heart disease, she decided to liquidate some of her money before the Nursing Homes could gobble it up. She gave each of my 4 siblings and I $10,000. My eldest sister Ledell took her family to Europe. Scott payed off some bills. Andy bought a Yurt to put on his land in Northern Wisconsin and my sister Sarah had her back yard professionally landscaped. And me?... I had a little fun, with my masculinity! I bought a "boys" bike and I decided to have Top Surgery. It was a hard decision. I mean, what was I supposed to get? A Bianchi or a Trek?

Having my breasts removed was one of the most pain free decisions that I have ever made. I never had any real struggles being a woman. I am a woman and I like being a woman. It's just that I embrace my masculinity, which is not necessarily a male thing. Just because I am masculine doesn't mean that I'm a man. My masculinity is just a part if what makes me, me.

Can't women be masculine without being perceived as men? Is masculinity only reserved for men and femininity only reserved for women? If a woman has a 20% breast reduction, is she 20% less female? Or 20% more male?

Anyway, lucky for me it was a pretty simple procedure. I went in, my breast tissue was removed and my nipples were carefully relocated onto my chest, and then I went home! There was no tread "good-bye" to my breasts and no great "welcoming" of my chest. I didn't feel as if I was shedding the "old" and welcoming in the "new". I just felt as if I was coming home. Coming home into my body, coming home into my self. My celebration has been and continues to be; a gentle smile upon my face, a sense of peace and a feeling of contentment...quite the display if emotion for a 4th generation Norwegian!

Some might say that I am Transgender, but really I'm not. For lack of a better term I use the words Gender Queer. But really, I'm just me.

I get "sirred" a lot and find myself being stared at in public restrooms quite often. Sometimes it doesn't bother me. But sometimes I just want to say to them: "Look at me! I'm a woman! I may not fit your idea if what a woman ought to look like. But get over it, and just let me go to the bathroom in peace!"

What hurts most though, is when people don't recognize or honor the masculinity that is a part of my womanhood. I am a woman, and there are no "buts" after that statement like, "I'm a woman, but I look like a man."

After all that has been said and done, really, I'm just me.

MOLLY
by AP Looze

(Lights come up on Andy, sitting on a stool at a high-top table. They are at a bar, with a can of Strongbow.)

Have I ever told you about Molly? She's, well, a former lover of mine. We were together for 20 years, give or take a few months, and she was pretty good to me, you know? I loved the way people would say her name, the way it was written on paper, and the way it felt like a pulse when people said it. Her mom called her Molldoll. She told me stories of her kindergarten teacher singing "Good Golly Miss Molly" whenever she laughed at a joke. She and her sister, Monica, went as the M&Ms for Halloween one year, and their mom went as the pack—like the keeper of two sweet treats. Her name fit her, and I still love it.

But Molly, well, she was tough on herself. She would become so weighted down with grief, even her own bones couldn't hold up her body. Her heart held her down with such a throttling force she couldn't get enough air to ask for help. I remember the times I spent by her side; I tried to coax her out of bed, but she resisted, becoming a lump of...sad on the mattress, heavy as wet sand. She never really told anyone, but she thought about suicide a lot. I tried to understand, but Molly wouldn't let me. I was there in her rampages. We'd get so angry at each other for simply existing, you know? I remember, once, we were in the kitchen, screaming, breathing so hard and with such force, tears bursting from our eyes like shrapnel. In our desperate heaves, she screamed I deserved to die. Waving a knife at my stomach, threatening to stab me I screamed back. "Fuck you, Molly! STOP." But she kept saying she'd do it, that she'd kill me, then turn the knife on herself. "Stop, stop stop!" I kept saying over and over again, holding her arms back from me. She got me on the wrist. I wear the scars as appendages of those memories. That was the last straw for her, I suppose, because later that night she swallowed every pill in her presence. I couldn't stop her. She laid them out in grid, and counted them, calculating her overdose like an equation for death. An ambulance took her to the hospital where she swallowed charcoal to absorb the toxins, but not the ones that were actually killing her.

We stayed together for some time after that, but sometimes, people, in being so close, grow apart like branches on a tree. It got to the point where I just *couldn't* with her...because I couldn't be with someone who kept causing me so much pain, no matter how good she was to me. Molly wasn't quite ready to hear that, but was understanding of the space we needed.

I was single for a time, and I must admit it was strange not having a companion, especially after 20 years of being with Molly.

And then, god, I started dating Ollie. *(laugh)* I know, right? They were cool, and we went on a few dates, but they weren't a good fit, and it jarred me when people would associate Ollie with me. I'd think: That's not who I'm with. We broke up after a few short and awkward months.

Without knowing what to do, I went back to Molly—out of desperation. She took me back in her arms with such warmth; she took care of me. We stayed together for a bit, mostly out of familiarity, but a certain distance had grown between us.

Then, in some serendipitous alignment of the stars, I met Andy. We were pretty shy with each other at first. It was new territory. I told Molly about them, and she was supportive, realizing that she and I really couldn't be primary partners anymore. Andy and I started flirting, and after a few months things got more serious, I started telling people about us — you know, just folks we trusted. Word eventually got around that we were together. But it's still hard. Andy is great, but they're not Molly.

Molly and I never officially broke up or anything — things just sort of led from one thing to the next until we weren't together anymore. I wonder sometimes if she'll appear in my life again. Will she greet me with warmth and flowers or with a knife and a suicide note? It's not like Andy isn't good enough, but finding them was a need. I learned a lot from being with Molly, though. I shouldn't yell or call people names and I should always treat loved ones kindly and with respect. Gosh, but I got to know her so well, you know? She's still...here. We're still legally together on paper—I don't think we'll officially part ways. I can't let go of something that was so good and bad to me, of Molly, of a name that truly stole my heart. And I'm learning that I don't have to. I don't have to let go.

NAKED²

by Anthony Neuman and Nicole Wilder

SHE: Skin

HE: Skin

SHE: So...

BOTH: Much..... skin.

HE: I was naked with you last night.

SHE: I was naked with you last night. I said "I'm nervous." You said you were nervous too.

HE: I took off my clothes—

SHE: Shyly asking permission to remove one barrier—then another.

HE: —you took off yours. We are exposed. In the light.

SHE: Finally, nothing but skin.

HE: Close

SHE: and love.

HE: Together

SHE: and wet.

HE: one.

SHE: and want.

HE: Your body pressed so deeply into mine that I'm no longer afraid of how it feels to be naked.

SHE: I want all of me touching all of you. I would crawl inside of you if I could.

HE: We are naked together

(beat.)

SHE: Can we enter each other simultaneously? Can we be each other's home? What would that mean? How will you let me in?

HE: My identity doesn't live between my legs. When I am sopping wet—dripping down my thighs. I am still a man. I am still a man when your fingers are inside of me.

SHE: It sounds like I'm equating intimacy with penetration, but it's not as crass as that. I don't mean to oversimplify... but currently it is what I crave.

HE: A man that wants to feel you inside of me. A man that has a space for you to fill.

SHE: Suddenly this need to not only envelope but to also be enveloped? If i'm not the only one opening my mouth, my legs, myself... if I enter you, am I suddenly clothed? Or do we become a mirror, reflecting the nakedness, vulnerability and openness of the other: naked squared.

(beat.)

HE: I lost my virginity last night

SHE: I lost my virginity last night

HE: I will never be the same

SHE: to an amazing man—

HE: she holds my cock in her hand. HOLDS MY COCK IN HER HAND.

SHE: —with a swollen cock—

60

HE: I feel like such a man. She yanks it, tugs it. Rolls her fingers across the swollen head. I can see her hand work my cock. SEE HER HAND WORK MY COCK. I can feel all of the ways that she wants me.

SHE: —and a pussy that welcomed my tentative fingers eagerly and graciously. Reaching inside of him felt like reaching inside of myself. No. Not felt like. Was.

HE: I didn't think I would redefine sex again. It's so easy to top someone and make them cum. I don't need to be present in my body for that. Until now. Now, I am present in my body the whole time. That means you are taking my body—I am giving you my body.

SHE: I feel power in the desire I see on his face... the need.

HE: I feel power when I am between your legs. When my arms are wrapped tightly around your smaller, slender, frame.

SHE: I can turn flesh into stone with a touch.

HE: When you mount my cock in an instinctual sort of way.

SHE: I can open the floodgates between his legs with a whisper.

HE: My fingers pulsing against the deepest of your insides.

SHE: I change the body of my lover, giving him power—

HE: Power.

SHE: —or showing him the definition of vulnerability as I see fit. *(beat.)* I have to redefine naked after being with you—

HE: I will never be the same

SHE: I am humbled by your willingness to let me touch
         you in places that have been the source of so much
         hurt and confusion.

HE: I don't even remember the same.

SHE: I am honored that you find me worthy to attempt to
         turn these places into sources of shared pleasure.

HE: I never want to be the same.

VOICEOVER

QUESTIONING BI
by Kelli Gorr

Why am attracted to butch women?
Is it because they look like men?

Am I the only woman who experiences the sensation of
wanting to have my own *real* giant cock when I'm naked with
another woman?

What constitutes sex between two women?

Am I having sex if I kiss her nipples, how 'bout her navel,
or if I suck her little toe repeatedly?

Surely if I am naked, kissing, and inserting fingers, that's sex,
right?

But at what exact moment? Where is the line?

Have you ever noticed how soft she is?
I have...

DISORDERED BODIES

by Kris Gebhard

Part 1

When I told my therapist I wanted to be a man,
I did not say I wanted hairy nipples.
I still don't want them but I'm growing
some kind of nipple hair garden under this shirt
so sometimes I try to hide it from the sun.
Sometimes for just a second I want to hide it from you
because it's not Christian Bale's chest.
But then I remind myself:
When I said I wanted to be a man,
I didn't actually wanna be a man,
I just needed some vindication
for the furnace I woke up inside of every morning,
and I knew the games I needed to play to get the 'scrip
were the same games folks of my type
have been playing since the '50s.

Back then they named us "transsexuals" so that
everybody else could be assured they were properly sexed.
Back then you had to get a letter from a doc explaining that
you were 'cross-dressing' because you were on your way to
surgeries, or the cops would arrest you.

I worry that nowadays we police ourselves:
Welcome to this disordered body.

Disbelieved disaster,
Diced and Divided,
Distributed and Dyslexic
Disease drenched and drudgerous, discontent –
Dysphoria: the cornerstone of gender identity disorder,
a severe disassociation from aspects of one's body
that relate to biological binary sex.

Let's dissect it:

When I told my therapist since I wasn't a woman
I guess I had to be a man,
I didn't know my melting skin could be of the holy ghost.
Thought my body had been
plumbed and electrified by a lunatic.
Hallway light switches turned on garbage disposals,
bathtub faucets flooded bedrooms.

I wasn't shameful, but I was desperate for resolution and my
therapist presented a male savior so I promised her
dysfunction.
Wept at least once a day.
Called it all dysphoria:
20 lashes before bed, front and back,
Therapists who patronize and doctors who fear,
30 sit ups and push ups repeat, check mirror, repeat,
A nurse who says I don't need a pap smear and shoves the
speculum so roughly inside me I am bruised afterwards,
Outlets set fire to toilets, clogged drains bottleneck and blow,
Being taken for 7 years younger than I am,
Maam'd and sir'ed and boy'd, she/he'd and it'd,
Knowing prison means solitary confinement
cuz they just don't know what else to do with us
Having my passport delayed for 9 months
because my genitals are an issue of national security
Daily counting the pronouns and sobbing
if the she's outweighed the he's
Blood staining every pair of my underwear because
I never expected to bleed there,
And sex.
Sex was a basement maze of concrete walls.
My first lover told me, as she wove her fingers into me,
it might hurt more than a tampon.
She had no idea how she pit stomach drop-kicked me.
We discovered a dwelling laced with booby traps
and highly sensitive smoke alarms.
I was unready and whimpered wounded, completely ashamed
that she had claimed some zone in my body I had,
(until her hands), believed did not exist.
Shortly after, I erased my womb.
Sealed it up. Began closet worshipping cock.
Hearing my own voice paralyzed me.

My first lover asked me to imagine who I wanted to look like.
I couldn't.
She went on:
"Well, if someday people think you're a dude,
you gotta tell 'em, 'I used to have a nice rack'".

Part 2

Is for all of us who embody dissonance,
All of us who absorb images of people like us
only in context of "transition,"
to some elusive and ridiculous ideal.
This is for all of us "disordered".
We are named "transgender" so that others
can preserve the illusion of being properly gendered.
We are named fat and defined as unhealthy so that others
 can pretend they are in health.
We are expected to starve or to purge
and it is even our friends who compliment our shrinking.
We are rewarded as long as we strive for gender perfection.
Many of us have terrible posture.
Maybe because we hunch to hide breasts,
or because we feel lacking,
or because they bring us the wrong kind of attention;
I think we've been taught who should stand.
Sometimes we try 4 or 5 or 12 outfits on in the morning and
when nothing fits it means we should stay in bed for the day,
but some days turn weeks or months
and prozac will trick you into indifferent jeans and t-shirts,
and if you're alive inside them maybe it's for the best.
Somedays we don't leave the house.
Sometimes we're petrified of grocery stores,
and malls, and Macy's, and Walmart, and changing rooms,
and mirrors— sometimes we shatter them,
sometimes we pray to them 25 times a day,
or turn off all the lights.
Sometimes we control our eating, sometimes it controls us.
Sometimes we can control our bleeding, sometimes we cannot.
Sometimes we bleed to control something,

anything that won't talk back.
And sometimes we have hidden the profoundness
of our naked bodies from even our closest lovers.

We fear because we know, we have all been pitied.
We have all been told, by someone or another,
that our "condition" is imagined.
That we should suck it up
and get on with it like the rest of them.
We have all been called traitors
Whether of race, or family, religion, money, fame,
or health, natural, or normal,
and gender,
gender is our most heinous betrayal.

We have been dogged.
We have been tagged too big, too tight, short, loud,
broad, thick, soft, fat, scared, weak, long, young, flashy,
flamboyant, hyper, extravagant, political, outspoken,
Too Much
Too Everything
And not enough, though the "not enough" is a short list:
Not feminine enough.
Not masculine enough.
For this, we endure much.
We are ripped and rung, kicked, fired, and evicted, prodded,
poked, laughed about, and ignored, beaten, and stolen.

At the bottom we ask, what of this body is mine to own?
What marrow remains after others have digested their fill?

When we do not know how to thrive, we cope.
We breathe shallow, we conform, we accessorize.
We surgery after surgery...
We dream of shedding these bodies.
We learn quickly how to bleach histories,
promise pathological, and fit in.
Passing is sheer reward.
We call it all "dysphoria" and search for the fix,
Doctors, therapists and dieticians extend prescriptions.
But for every one of us who disappears their differentness
to assimilate to absurdity,

those of us who cannot disappear must pay the consequences.

Dysphoria is the ax swinging back
and knocking you unconscious.
The block of wood: your beauty.
Stop trying to split it into two genders.
Can't you see?
We are splinters of each other.

We are all warriors
Healers
Magicians
Teachers
Prophets
When our bodies seem strangers to our souls,
we must learn from each other how to breathe.
Summon our sacks of mucus and blood,
muscle our mountains upon backs and journey.

This is a claiming:

Thank Goddess for our bodies, all disarranged as they seem.
We are an eco-system of pumping, flowing,
beating, moaning, yelping, exclaiming:
Claim this chaos!

When your skin feels like
somebody else's wrinkled cotton sheets,
When the gym is your purgatory,
When you chisel a sculpture to crawl into
instead of a fountain to dance within,
Claim soft.
Claim oil and water dressing your body in comfort.
Claim fat, claim fortunate.
When you harden too easily,
Claim muscled elegance.
Claim space, whether your physicality requires it
or longs for it.
When you buy the wrong sized bra on purpose,
When you cry in dressing rooms,
When you won't let anyone shop with you,
Claim every department in the stupid store.

When no one carries your shoe size, or anything size,
Screw size,
Start a sewing collective and clothe our flows righteous.
Or find somebody who ships free
and send it back as many times as it takes.
When razors ride rigid and you're sick of shaving every day,
Claim hair—hairy faces, hairy vulvas,
hairy inner thighs, and hairy asses,
nose hairs, leg hairs, and armpit hairs.
When binders sweat and squeeze you,
Claim flabby, flopping tits.
When every hallway blessed by your lover's hands
is decked with flashing exit signs,
Claim flaccid dicks.
Claim silicone, leather, and lube—
Honey, claim lots of lube.
When you laugh and they don't get it,
Claim smiles, winks, and teeth.
When pitch is the sole determinant of a Ma'am or a Sir,
Claim booming, and raspy, chirpy, and squeaky,
squealing, and thunderous, excited, and filled-with-passion,
and filled-with-courage, and
Bathrooms—claim every fucking stall, urinal, and toilet.
Claim childhood, every moment you felt unsafe,
and every day you chose your own clothes,
imagine yourself with perfect posture,
because children are taught
how to slump in their chairs by adults.
Imagine yourself with perfect gender,
because children are taught.
Claim ecology of bodies, it takes yours to give mine meaning
(so baby make me look good).
When you don't know if they're afraid to sleep with you,
or if you're afraid to sleep with you,
When it's easier to undress others than to dress yourself,
Claim the challenge—because you will never know
how many people you free just by putting on your
favorite fancy pants, and skirts, and scarves, and
metal through skin, and glitter, and ink, and femme,
boi, butch, dyke, fag, queen, queer, king, pansy, pussy,
bottom, daddy, bear, twink, flaming, and fabulous!
Claim it all at once!

Claim pleasure, and the 2,735 places on our bodies
that are pleasurable to touch, tantalize, torture, and tease.
Claim ears, and shoulders, and armpits, and eyelashes,
and the insides of knees, and big toes and little toes,
and calves, and hips, and tongues, and lips, and nipples,
and fingers and wrist and hands, and teeth, and tongues,
and hands, and lips, and tongues, and hands.
Claim gorgeous, handsome, charming, adorable,
damn fucking sexy.
Claim pronouns—claim all the pronouns,
or none of the pronouns,
refuse to claim and make them deal with their confusion.

If you cannot tell me what name
will curve your flesh home,
I refer to you as dazzling.

If you cannot tell me what cloth
will cradle your skin safe,
I dress you in wonder.

*(Performers from other pieces in the show start to quietly join
him onstage, as themselves — no costumes.)*

When you are too tired to shout
for the 434th time at the bully,
link arms with us.
We roll millions deep.
We are yelling "red rover"
and anyone who wants to can join our line.

There is nothing more dangerous
than loving ourselves exactly as we are.

We are may be terrified,
but this is our time.

Beauty:

This is our time.

END OF PLAY

Helpful Terms

(some borrowed with love from the Transgender Commission at the UofM - http://www.glbta.umn.edu/trans/)

Assigned Sex At Birth: At birth, infants are assigned a sex based on a combination of bodily characteristics including chromosomes, hormones, internal reproductive organs, and genitals.

Cisgender(ed): The opposite of transgender – someone who identifies today as the sex they were assigned at birth.

FTM (Female-to-Male): Literally "female-to-male", a person assigned female sex and feminine gender at birth who is either transitioning into a male identity and/or body, or who identifies as an FTM transperson, transman, or transsexual.

Gender: We define gender as a system of meanings and symbols and the rules, privileges and punishments for their use. All the ways in which people express their bodies and communicate with the world can be gendered and encoded with meaning—for example: vocal inflection, body hair, clothing, laughter, sexuality, and the very space one takes up in a room.

Gender Expression: The external representation of one's gender identity, usually expressed through feminine or masculine behaviors and signals such as clothing, hair, movement, voice or body characteristics. Transgender people often seek to match their gender expression with their self-affirmed gender identity, rather than their birth-assigned gender.

Gender Identity: One's internal sense of who they are; being a woman or man, girl or boy, or between or beyond these genders.

Gender Identity Disorder (GID): A controversial DSM-IV diagnosis given to transgender and other gender-variant people. Because it labels people as "disordered", Gender Identity Disorder is often considered offensive. The diagnosis is frequently given to children who don't obey expected norms in terms of dress, play or behavior. Such children are often subjected to intense psychotherapy, behavior modification and/or institutionalization. This replaces the outdated term "gender dysphoria".

Gender Variant/Gender Non-Conforming: A person who does not conform to gender-based expectations of society (including transgender, transsexual, intersex, genderqueer, cross-dresser, etc.)

Genderqueer: A gender variant person whose gender identity is neither male nor female, is between or beyond genders, or is some combination of genders, in terms of expression and/or identity.

MTF (Male-to-Female): Literally "male-to-female", a person assigned male sex and masculine gender at birth who is either transitioning into a female identity and/or body, or who identifies as an MTF transperson, transwoman, or transsexual.

Pronouns: A replacement word for the subject – she/her, he/him. Some transgender or gender non-conforming individuals choose to use gender-neutral pronouns such as they/them or ze/hir.

Queer: An umbrella term for sexual minorities that are not heterosexual, nor related to gender-binary. Some people who identify as queer may be trying to separate themselves from discourse, ideologies, and lifestyles that typify mainstream LGBT communities as being oppressive or assimilationist. Some use the term because "bi-sexual" is too limiting.

Transgender: An umbrella term for people whose gender identity and/or expression differs from the gender they were assigned at birth or from what is culturally validated. Trans people choose many words to describe themselves and/or their communities, including but not limited to: transsexual, genderqueer, Two Spirit, FTM, MTF, drag queen or king, cross dresser, gender non-conforming, gender variant, woman, and man.

Trans*: When you see "trans*" in print, this shortened, asterisked word generally refers to a group of people that includes transgender and gender non-conforming individuals.

Transition: Refers to the complex process of altering one's gender, which may include some, all or none of the following: changing name and/or sex on legal documents; hormone therapy; and chest, facial and/or genital alteration. Transgender people may or may not choose to alter their bodies.

Transsexual: A person whose intent is to live as a gender other than that assigned at birth. Most transsexuals engage in some process of altering either primary or secondary sexual characteristics, through hormone treatment or surgery or both. Some transsexuals live full time in their chosen gender without any alteration to physiology.

Transphobia: The fear and hatred of or the discomfort with people who identify or may be perceived to be transgender, respectively. Transphobic reactions often lead to intolerance, bigotry, and violence against anyone not perceived to match gender norms. Transphobia is not homophobia, yet they do have a connection. Stereotypes of the lesbian and gay communities are often based on gender expressions and/or roles within a binary gender system in a monosexual (hetero, gay, lesbian) paradigm (i.e. gay men as effeminate, lesbians as masculine, etc). Since trans-identified folks transgress a binary gender system, they may be more susceptible to homophobic actions.

Made in the USA
Charleston, SC
16 June 2012